Mastering Calm

Powerful Stress Releasing Techniques for
Enhanced Health and Well-Being
Christina Concord

Funky Munky Publishing Company

© Copyright Christina Concord 2023 - All rights reserved.

Cover Photo Credit: © Copyright Cover Christina Concord 2021 – All rights reserved.

The content contained within this book may not be reproduced, duplicated or transmitted without direct written permission from the author or the publisher.

Under no circumstances will any blame or legal responsibility be held against the publisher, or author, for any damages, reparation, or monetary loss due to the information contained within this book. Either directly or indirectly. You are responsible for your own choices, actions, and results.

Legal Notice:

This book is copyright protected. This book is only for personal use. You cannot amend, distribute, sell, use, quote or paraphrase any part, or the content within this book, without the consent of the author or publisher.

Disclaimer Notice:

Please note the information contained within this document is for educational and entertainment purposes only. All effort has been executed to present accurate, up to date, and reliable, complete information. No warranties of any kind are declared or implied. Readers acknowledge that the author is not engaging in the rendering of legal, financial, medical or professional advice. The content within this book has been derived from various sources. Please consult a licensed professional before attempting any techniques outlined in this book.

By reading this document, the reader agrees that under no circumstances is the author responsible for any losses, direct or indirect, which are incurred as a result of the use of the information contained within this document, including, but not limited to, — errors, omissions, or inaccuracies.

Published by: Funky Munky Publishing Company, LLC

For Andrew,

You are my rock and my biggest supporter. Thank you for always being there for me - for making me laugh through the hard times and cheering me on when I don't think I can move forward. I am forever grateful for you and will always love you forever, and ever.

***

Contents

Introduction	VI
1. Foundation of Relaxation	1
2. Creating a Personal Sanctuary	6
3. Mental Strategies to Release Stress	10
4. Emotional Strategies to Release Stress	20
5. Physical Strategies to Release Stress	26
6. Daily Rituals for A Balanced Life	33
7. Integrating Calm Into Your Life	41
Conclusion	46
References	47

Introduction

Stress. We all know what it is. At some point in our lives, we all have experienced it. Heck, you might be stressed at this moment, right now!

Stress, as inevitable as it is, is a completely normal reaction that occurs whenever you are exposed to stressful circumstances. For example, stress happens when we start to feel the pressure from the responsibilities we have in our lives, family, jobs, etc. Since it is bound to happen, our bodies are designed to react to it.

In fact, some stress you experience can be known as "good stress", called *eustress*. *Eustress* is a form of positive stress you feel when you are excited and motivated to perform well in a situation. For example, eustress is the anxious kind stress you experience when you are about to go on vacation, and you are excited about the journey to a foreign place. Another example of "good stress" is when you start a new job or begin to learn a new hobby. These are examples of short-lived stress that don't last long for you as the nervous stress is likely to subside.

It's when you experience constant, long-term stress that is not good for your health. This type of "bad stress" is called *distress*. When *distress* symptoms are ignored, this type of "bad stress" can do a lot of harm to our bodies and can lead to problems with our overall health and well-being.

Depression. Heart disease. High blood pressure. Obesity. Stroke. These are some of the conditions that can result when you are chronically stressed and do not take action to manage your stress levels.

During times when you feel distressed – and even being proactive to take action *before* you experience distress – it is important to take a few moments to relax and take care of *you*. We all need to start being mindful about how we can manage our stress levels so we do not stay stressed, because as I mentioned, staying stressed is what causes damage to our overall well-being.

In fact, it's best for you to incorporate "self-care" measures into your day-to-day life so managing "bad stress" will be easier for you when stressful situations do arise. I like to call these "self-care" measures, "*Stress Releasing*". A way to "release" stress so that it is not a part of you anymore, so you don't hang onto it and so you can set it free.

That's why I am writing this book, to give others quick techniques to release stress so they can have quick strategies in their back pocket for the times when they need to be calm and destress. In this book, my plan is to guide you through the basics of stress and its impact on your overall health and well-being. Next, we will explore strategies for releasing stress and then we will develop a personalized and sustainable plan to manage your stress better.

I may not be a professional in stress management (it's always best to talk to your doctor if you feel you are chronically stressed and need to manage your stress levels), but I have researched stress relief extensively in order to work every day to prevent myself from being chronically stressed about situations in my life.

Another reason I am writing this book is I am also a firm believer that everyone should take their health seriously and work at making a better version of themselves, every day, even if the progress is made with the smallest amount. I figured that if I could write this short book with strategies that help me, I can help others, too, even if I only help one person.

CHAPTER ONE

Foundation of Relaxation

"You don't find your ground by looking for stability. You find your ground by relaxing into instability." — Cory Muscara, founder of the Long Island Center for Mindfulness

***

The Science of Stress: Understanding Stress Responses and How Relaxation Counteracts Stress

When you are in a stressful or overwhelming situation, stress hormones are triggered and your heart may start pounding, your muscles may start to tense, and you may start breathing faster. These feelings, or reactions are also known as the "fight-or-flight" response.

Here, you are in "survival" mode – meaning it is in your nature to react to a life-threatening situation. While the stressful or overwhelming situation may not actually be life threatening, this is how your body responds:

While there are a lot of brain functions that go on, in a nutshell, the brain responds to a stressful situation by initiating a complex reaction involving the amygdala and the hypothalamus in your brain. The amygdala sends distress signals to the hypothalamus – the command center of your brain that communicates with the rest of your body through the autonomic nervous system – alerting your body to make a decision: do you resist or run away?

Your autonomic nervous system has two parts: the sympathetic nervous system (SNS) and the parasympathetic nervous system (PNS). The SNS is your stress response system. It's like a gas pedal that triggers the release of adrenaline (a stress related hormone) from your adrenal glands and increases your heart rate, blood pressure and energy in response to danger.

The PNS is like the brakes. It calms your body down after the danger is over. If the danger persists, the hypothalamus keeps the body on alert by releasing cortisol (another stress related hormone). Only once the "threat" is gone do your cortisol levels decrease, and the PNS reduces the stress response.

Therefore, over time when you are chronically stressed, it starts to take a toll on your body. As mentioned before, chronic stress can contribute to high blood pressure, it can promote the formation of artery-clogging deposits and can cause changes in your brain that play a role in anxiety, depression, and addiction.

This is why it is important to relax and incorporate relaxation techniques into your daily routine. Relaxation techniques literally counteract stress because your body's "relaxation response" is the exact opposite of your body's stress response – you breathe slower, which lowers your blood pressure, which lowers your heart rate. This calms your body, overall, so that it is not in the shocking state it is in when it is responding to stress.

Mindfulness and Mental Clarity: The Role of Awareness in Stress Management

While chronic stress can impair the body's immune system and can play a part in making other health problems worse, you can play a part in lowering your body's stress response. According to the American Psychological Association, researchers believe there are benefits to mindfulness that have an ability to lower the body's response to stress.

When you are being mindful, you start to live in the present moment and become aware of things that are going on in front of you, now. According to the Mirriam-Webster Dictionary, mindfulness is "the practice of maintaining a nonjudgmental state of heightened or complete awareness of one's thoughts, emotions, or experiences on a moment-to-moment basis".

In the case of stress, this means that you start to become aware of your thoughts, emotions, and behaviors when your body is in the fight-or-flight response. Once you notice these indicators that you are in fight-or-flight response, you can "catch" yourself in the moment and take action to resolve or manage your stress levels better.

"If you are depressed you are living in the past.
If you are anxious you are living in the future.
If you are at peace you are living in the present."
-Lao Tzu

Techniques for Mindful Living

According to the Mayo Clinic, "mindfulness is a type of meditation in which you focus on being intensely aware of what you're sensing and feeling in the moment, without interpretation or judgement."

To practice mindfulness, there are many different meditation techniques that you can perform. One of the most beneficial things you can do is take the time to sit down, be present and pay attention.

In a busy world that seems to keep picking up pace every day, it is a good practice to slow yourself down. Sit in a quiet place, take a few deep breaths, and start to notice the things around you. Are you warm? Are you cold? What noises do you hear? Pay attention to the little things around you.

If you are drinking coffee or tea, take time to smell, sip, taste and enjoy the beverage you are drinking. If you are eating, use the same practice and enjoy the food you are eating. This is the same practice as living in the moment and fully experiencing the thing you are doing right now at this moment.

Focusing on your breathing is also very important. We will talk more about breathing techniques in the chapters that come. But, simply sitting there and taking a deep beath with your eyes closed can help you "slow things down" and take a minute for yourself.

Sometimes, a quick meditation can help you accomplish this, too. In future chapters, we will discuss different types of meditations that you can do to help you become more mindful, present, and calm.

CHAPTER TWO

Creating a Personal Sanctuary

"Your personal space is a sacred place where you can find peace and regain your sense of self." -Unknown

***

Your personal space has everything to do with your stress levels, so I want to talk about some things that I do to make sure that my own personal space is a space that isn't contributing to my stress levels.

First, I want to mention that anything you need to do to make your personal space or home peaceful to yourself – from how you decorate your house to the furniture you have – can make a big impact on how you feel when you occupy your own personal space.

Decluttering Your Space

The first thing that I do if I feel overwhelmed is clean. I realize that not everyone is like me, and cleaning may not be your "go-to" when you feel overwhelmed. But, if you are like me and think that tidying up makes you feel better, go for it!

I don't always thoroughly, "clean-clean", as I call it. Rather, sometimes picking up clutter around the house and putting it where it belongs is all it takes. There is something about feeling like everything is organized and in its place that makes my stress levels subside.

It's also not always about taking out the broom, dustpan, mop, and cleaning supplies, either. Maybe I need to purge my space and throw things out that no longer make me feel happy? At least once a year I go through my clothes and donate ones that I no longer use or like anymore.

Or maybe I feel like there is some stagnant energy in my house and I decided to clean out a closet or go through a box of old whatever-is-inside of it to purge things that I no longer need in my life.

Other times, working on a project to keep my mind occupied does the trick. Like, working on a project off of the old "house-fixes-to-do" list.

Anything that helps me declutter, organize, or clean-up will sometimes take my mind off of my stressful situations, help me calm myself down and forget all about it.

Aromatherapy

The fragrant smell of a home-cooked meal. The strong, rich, warm aroma of coffee roasting in the morning. There's always a good feeling that happens after you smell something good.

Enter, aromatherapy. According to Johns Hopkins Medicine, "[a]romatherapy is the practice of using essential oils for therapeutic benefit...When inhaled, the scent molecules in essential oils travel from the olfactory nerves directly to the brain and especially impact the amygdala, the emotional center of the brain."

You can also use essential oils topically by adding a drop or two to your skin.

Essential oils are good if you are looking for natural remedies for certain ailments you may have. In terms of stress releasing, essential oils like lavender, or eucalyptus can have a calming effect when you inhale them.

Before I go to bed, I have a roller ball with lavender essential oil in it that I inhale before bed. First, I roll the oil on one of my wrists. Rub my wrists together, then breathe in the scent. This relaxes me and helps me have a more peaceful sleep.

Sometimes, I use eucalyptus if I've had a really stressful day, as some research has shown that eucalyptus oil reduces activity in your SNS and may reduce stress and anxiety.

Make Your Home a Happy Home

The things suggested here are only a few things you can do to make your own personal space into your own personal sanctuary. If it means doing something big like repainting a wall or two or buying a new comfy chair, or adding little touches like photos, artwork, or candles to your space, you should make it happen.

Your personal space should be as warm and welcoming to you and make you feel like you can fade away from the stresses of the world inside your own personal space.

Chapter Three

Mental Strategies to Release Stress

"Linger in the space between thoughts and discover what stillness has to offer."
-Calm App Reflection

***

Have you ever felt like your brain is on overload? Like your "brain hurts", sometimes? Typically, this happens after you've been thinking a lot, when you have been concentrating for long periods of time or those times when you feel like you're going a "million miles a minute".

This is usually a good time to take a cognitive break. Cognitive breaks are good to take because your mind needs to rest. When you give your mind a rest, taking a minute, or two (or five) will help you de-stress and give your mind a chance to relax and you will be able to think more clearly.

While some studies have proven that quietly sitting in a dark place for 10 minutes or more can help your mind relax, I'll give you some other techniques that have been proven effective to calm your mind.

The Healing Power of the Outdoors

While we talked about creating your own personal space inside your home, being outdoors can be relaxing, too. In fact, being outdoors can reduce stress, lower cortisol levels, and improve your mood.

Since we were just on the topic of personal spaces, creating a space in your backyard or somewhere outside of your home where you can sit and relax can be a huge stress releaser. The smell of fresh air, a warm breeze on a hot day, the chill in the air on a fall day…there is something warm, cozy, and refreshing about sitting outside and being in nature that helps me release stress.

If you don't want to create a space, or don't have an outdoor space, you can always take a walk or go to a nearby park. Taking walks is not only good for your health, physically, but it is also good for your mental health, too.

Whether you choose to be outside in your own backyard sanctuary or if you choose to take walks frequently, being outside is extremely healing and restorative, and aids in your well-being. Not only does being in nature calm your nervous system and reduce stress, but it also reduces cortisol and adrenaline levels, and lowers your blood pressure.

Utilizing Breath to Release Stress

Using your breath for stress relief is a very powerful and effective technique to release stress. This can be as simple as taking time to breathe. It sounds funny, but if you're anything like me, there are times throughout your day where you catch yourself holding your breath!

This is where it is important to be mindful of your actions and how your body is responding throughout your day. In my case, if I notice that I am holding my breath, I take a minute to just *breathe*. I take my focus off whatever task I am working on, sit down if I'm standing, close my eyes and turn my focus to my breath, paying attention to my *in* breath and my *out* breath.

Deep, slow breathing not only helps you relax but it can also help you lower your heart rate and your blood pressure. One of my favorite slow breathing techniques is a technique used by Navy Seals to quickly get their nervous system under control, called *Box Breathing*. Box Breathing helps you stay focused while reducing stress and improving your overall well-being. Here's how to do it:

1. Breathe in for four seconds, counting slowly, as you feel air entering your lungs.

2. Hold your breath for four seconds.

3. Exhale, slowly, for four seconds through your mouth.

4. Repeat steps one through three for as long as you need to regain your focus and feel the stress release from your body.

Another breathing method that is effective in helping you release stress (and sleep better) is the *4-7-8 breathing technique*. Here's how to do this one:

1. Slowly breathe in for four seconds as you feel air entering your lungs.

2. Hold your breath for seven seconds.

3. Exhale, slowly through your mouth, for eight seconds.

4. Repeat steps one through three for as long as you need to regain your focus and feel the stress release from your body and/or until you fall asleep.

Meditation

Meditation is a great way to "get away" for a few minutes. To focus on your breath and not everything else around you, to calm yourself down. We briefly talked about mindful meditation, but there are various ways you can meditate. My favorite type of meditation to do that relaxes me is to just sit with myself for 20 minutes and just breathe. That's it. With this type of meditation, it helps me focus inwardly to help me reduce stress.

This is how I meditate:

- I sit in my favorite chair and make sure I am comfortable. You can also choose to lie down if it makes you more comfortable.

- I set a timer for 20 minutes, close my eyes and just breathe.

Tips for this type of meditation:

- Make sure that the alarm noise on your timer is not a jarring noise. On my phone, I have a "fade in" type of alarm where the noise gradually increases the volume. I also make sure it is a pleasant sound instead of an annoying buzzing sound. It helps me come out of my meditation easier and also contributes to the relaxation I am trying to achieve.

- It takes patience to start this type of meditation as sitting alone with your thoughts, when the goal is to *not think*, is not as easy as you would think. Give yourself some grace while you are working at not thinking. Thoughts will enter your head! Whenever they do, push them to the side and try to think of a blank space while you turn your thoughts back to your breath. Focusing on your in breath and out breath can help you push thoughts away, easier.

- If 20 minutes is too much for you to sit and meditate, start with five minutes and work your way up to 10 minutes, and then, finally 20 minutes. If you want to meditate for longer (say 30 minutes or longer) go for it! This is your time to relax.

- Play some calming, "spa" music or softer music to listen to as background noise while you meditate. You don't want to listen to music with lyrics as you will more than likely sing along in your head.

Another form of meditation is *Guided Imagery Meditation*. With this type of meditation, you don't have to push your thoughts away. Instead, you can use visualization and daydreaming skills. This is a little bit easier than straight meditating.

Here is how to meditate with Guided Imagery:

- Sit somewhere comfortable, or lie down.

- Close your eyes and imagine you are somewhere that has relaxing and calming scenery to you. For example, you could be in a forest, a beach, the mountains. Wherever is most calming to you.

- Pay attention to your senses and think about what you see, hear, feel, smell and taste. Use the Mindfulness practices we talked about and really "live" in the moment you are imagining.

- Set a timer (remember one that won't be jarring when you are through) for 20 minutes.

If you're looking for an easier, quicker meditation that involves imagery, another imagery meditation technique is called "Palming".

This one is quicker:

- Sit in a comfortable position or lie down.

- Cover your eyes with the palms of your hands.
- Visualize a color you think of when you think of being stressed.
- Change the color to a more relaxing color, such as blue (unless you associate "blue" with stress).

Meditation takes practice and the more you meditate, the better you get with it. If you are new to meditation, it can take some time to get into the flow. Make sure you give yourself some grace and don't stress yourself out over getting it "perfect".

Taking a Bath

A warm bath can soothe the muscles and provide a quiet, solitary space. If you're not a bath person, standing in the shower and allowing the warm water to rush over your head while you stand still and breathe, can be calming as well.

Whether you are taking a bath or a shower, to me, it's all about the *experience*. I recommend giving yourself as much of a spa experience as you can!

- If you can, dim the lights.
- Light some candles.
- Play some soft, calming music.
- Be mindful during the experience and live in the moment. *Feel* the temperature of the water, *smell* the scent of the

candles or bath bubbles, *listen* to the music, *immerse* yourself in the experience and *take your time*.

- After you are finished in the bath or shower, don't rush out of the bathroom, take some time to sit and relax before getting dressed. Or, get dressed in your comfiest and coziest clothing to sit and relax after your bath or shower.

- You can also choose to sit in a bathrobe or a towel, afterwards. I recommend using Turkish towels as they are the most soft and luxurious towels on the market. If you don't have Turkish towels, that's ok! The bath towels you have will be just fine. Or, as I mentioned, you can put on your robe.

Again, make an experience of it. One that will work to release stress from your body and make you feel calm.

Watching Movies or Listening to Music to Release Stress

Sometimes, sitting down in your favorite spot to take time out of your day to make yourself comfortable – maybe cuddled up with your favorite blankets – to watch a movie helps you release stress.

It doesn't matter the particular type of movie you watch, as long as the movie is one of *your* favorite genres to watch. Watching a movie that you find entertaining allows you to take your mind off of the stresses of your life.

Not a fan of movies? It happens. Sitting in your favorite, comfortable spot in your home, or sitting outside while you listen to music can also help take the stresses of the day away. Heck! You can be anywhere and listen to music, just as long as it is music that is relaxing to *you*.

It has been known that music can influence your mood as much as your mood can influence the music choices you make. In terms of trying to release stress, calming, smooth music has been known to quiet your mind, help you to focus, relax your muscles and calm down your nervous system.

While I have read that music with a slower tempo is best to listen to in order to soothe and calm you down (and have also experienced this feeling when I listen to smooth jazz, "spa" music or classical music), not everyone likes that type of music.

If your favorite music is not the type of music I mentioned, don't listen to it. It is better to listen to your favorite type of music than try to force yourself to listen to music you don't like. Listening to music you don't like can actually create more tension in your body, aggravate you and cause the reverse effect of what you are trying to accomplish.

If you're not sure what to listen to, here are various sounds that have been known to release stress from your body. According to the University of Nevada, Reno Counseling Services, "Native American, Celtic, Indian stringed-instruments, drums, and flutes are very effective at relaxing the mind even when played moderately loud. Sounds of rain, thunder, and nature sounds may also be relaxing particularly when mixed with other music, such as light jazz, classical (the "largo" movement), and easy listening music.".

I have also heard that Reggae Music and even Heavy Metal Music (yes, research has shown that Heavy Metal Music can help lower your blood pressure). Some others I like to listen to are "Spa" music. Take time to listen to different variations to see if they help calm you down.

Reading

Escaping the world through movies is one thing, but burying yourself in a good book can also help you release stress. There is something about opening a book and flipping through the pages to immerse yourself into a whole new world. Not only can this be a great escape from the stressors in your life, but it is also a very beneficial relaxation technique. It also helps to relax you when you cozy yourself up with a warm blanket while sitting in your favorite spot in the house.

I know in our digital world that some people read eBooks, and that's totally ok if that is your style. For me, I need the physical copy in my hand to fully enjoy the story I am reading.

CHAPTER FOUR

Emotional Strategies to Release Stress

"It's not stress that kills us, it's our reaction to it." -Hans Selye

***

When life is chaotic, you may feel a wave of emotions building up inside of you. This is another indicator that it would be best for you to step away and give yourself a chance to breathe.

When you feel this buildup of emotions, it is good to find an outlet for these emotions to escape. As they escape, you will be able to release the stress that comes along with these emotions, too.

Creativity

Allowing your creativity to flow can help occupy your mind and take stressors of your day away. Creative activities really do take your mind away from things and allow you to express yourself however you choose. There are no rules or boundaries to creativity, and you have complete freedom. To me that *screams* stress relief!

While a creative activity can also be a form of meditation and being mindful, being creative can also benefit our health aside from releasing stress from our bodies. Being creative has been shown to reduce cortisol levels, help us relax, improve concentration, and help our overall well-being. In general, being creative is a pleasant and healthy distraction we can exhibit to release stress.

Perhaps you choose to invest your creative energy into a hobby or a craft? Taking up a hobby or craft is a good way to take your mind off the stressors of life. This is because the activity you are choosing is occupying your mind on the task at hand and at the same time allows you to use your creative energy.

I like to think of hobbies as progressive types of activities that involve the "completion" of something. When you finish working on your hobby, you are more likely to feel a sense of achievement and self-satisfaction. At this point, your body releases endorphins - the body's "feel-good" chemicals – helping you to improve your mood.

One of my favorite things to do is color in an "Adult Coloring Book". I also like doing puzzles. Crossword Puzzles, Sudoku, Word Searches, and other Problem-Solving Puzzles because they help me relax while engaging my brain at the same time. Plus, problem-solving activities help improve cognitive skills on top of the other benefits creativity brings.

Journaling and Self-Reflection

Ever since I was six years old, I have written in a journal. As I got older and read pages that I had written, and while I wrote about the good stuff, I noticed that most of the time, I was writing about things that were stressful to me in my life.

After learning that writing down your thoughts and feelings can help you understand and manage them better, I realized that I wrote about my stressors to get them on paper and out of my head. Not only did writing help me organize my thoughts, it helped me come to conclusions about the stressors in my life to essentially solve my own problem. I realized this is good for me, so I continue to journal at least once a week to make sure my thoughts are in order.

You don't have to journal every day or every week but journaling at least once a month can help you release stress and gain clarity on your current state of mind.

It doesn't matter how much or how little you write, if you write down your thoughts and feelings, journaling can help you release stress. If you're not sure where to start, here are some journal prompts that may help kickstart your writing:

- What are one or two stressors that happened over the past few days? How did you overcome them?
- Write down at least three things you are grateful for.
- What is your favorite activity to help you destress?
- Do you find your job stressful? What are some aspects

that make it stressful? Or not?

- What is your favorite inspirational quote? What is it about the quote that makes it your favorite?

- What is one challenging situation you are going through right now?

- When do you feel the most relaxed?

- Describe your ideal vacation.

- What is one thing you can do today to make your life less stressful?

- What is one positive thing that happened today?

Napping

I was always afraid to take naps because I thought I would sleep throughout my entire day and miss out. However, I learned that taking a short nap can be one of the best ways to reset your stress levels.

According to Landmark Health, "[naps] lower stress and help to regulate mood, reducing anxiety and depression and inducing relaxation.". If I need to take a nap, I typically take a short nap for 20 minutes.

This is because 20 minutes gives you just enough sleep for you to get some rest without putting you into a deep sleep. You don't want to enter deep sleep because when you wake up from a deep sleep, you will be groggy and want to go back to sleep.

In these short 20 minutes, I wake up feeling refreshed and ready to continue my day, without feeling like I slept through my day.

The Power of Social Connections

Socializing can be very healing and can also help you release stress when you have the opportunity to spend time with friends, loved ones and even strangers. Especially, if the people you are around make you feel good from spending time with them.

If you don't have the time to spend time with family or friends, calling them on the phone to catch up can do wonders to relieve your stress levels.

I mentioned "strangers" because I own a few businesses and meeting and talking to strangers is part of my job. Meeting new people can be a pleasant experience. Plus, I've always felt, the more people you know, the more you learn new things and get to experience their worlds that you may not be familiar with.

Perhaps you are in line at the grocery store and talk to the people around you.? This is an example of an opportunity to socialize or briefly chat with someone that helps improve your overall mood.

Humor and Laughter

Speaking of socializing, sometimes you get the added benefit of laughing with friends, family and even strangers. When they say laughter is one of the best medicines, there may be something to that. Not only does laughter release physical tension in your body and helps to decrease stress hormones, it also releases endorphins, allowing you to release overall stress.

It's always good to find something every day to make you laugh. Whether you watch a funny movie, go to a comedy show (or watching a comedy special on Netflix), watch a funny YouTube video, seek to hear a funny joke, or spend time with some friends, these are some things you can do to help make yourself laugh to help your overall health and well-being.

Whenever I can't find anything to laugh at, I like to tell myself a joke I heard a long time ago that still makes me laugh to this day. It may be a "dad joke", but maybe it can help brighten your day?

What do you call a bear with no teeth?

A Gummy Bear.

I'm not sure who came up with that joke, but I think it's one for the books. At least my books because it reminds me that it's important to find humor in the little things, too. What's the last funny thing you've seen, or funny joke you've heard that made you laugh?

As long as you make sure you laugh every day, you will be able to release stress and improve your overall well-being. According to HelpGuide.org, "[a] good, hearty laugh relieves physical tension and stress, leaving your muscles relaxed for up to 45 minutes.". So yeah. Laughter is *that* important.

Chapter Five

Physical Strategies to Release Stress

"Exercise is the key not only to physical health but to peace of mind." -Nelson Mandela

***

Have you ever felt like you have some pent-up energy building up inside of you, and feel the need to blow off some steam? When you need more than a mental or emotional break and feel like the ton of energy inside your body needs to be released, this is a good indication that you need to get up and move! Most physical activities have the added benefits of mental and/or emotional releases, too.

A Word About Movement

When you are stressed, an easy thing to do is get up and start *moving*...anything to get your body moving can not only be beneficial for your physical health (and mental and/or emotional health), but it can also be helpful to release stress and to improve your overall well-being.

When I say move, I'm not talking about full blown exercising (*yet*). I'm talking about small movements such as taking a walk, climbing stairs, cleaning the house and perhaps even some Yoga (more to come on this). If you are not used to moving, you have to walk before you can run (no pun intended!) so starting with the smaller tasks can help you build up to moving in ways that work for you.

Physical Engagement (Exercising)

One of the best ways to engage physically is to create an exercise routine. In order to start a successful exercise routine, it is **always best to consult with your doctor**. Especially if you have not exercised in a while or have health concerns that may need to be addressed with a professional.

Not only does exercising help you physically, but it also helps to boost your mood by releasing endorphins and increasing your self-esteem. Exercise can also help you focus and clear your mind, helping you with the mental aspect of stress relief.

I'm not going to give you an exercise routine that you can't keep up with or may think is too easy for you. What I have learned about exercising is to do *what you have fun with*. It doesn't make sense to make exercising a "chore", especially since it is something we *all* need to do to keep our bodies in great shape. You might as well do something that doesn't feel like work!

For me, I like to swim. I can do laps for hours when I get going. This is not only because I love to do it, doing laps is like a meditative process to me. When I do laps, I am able to "turn my brain off", focus on my breath and just swim.

When I am unable to go swimming, I like to practice Barre, Yoga and Kickboxing. I also have a rowing machine which helps give me a total body workout on the days that I don't have a lot of time to fully workout.

Walking is also one of my favorite activities and I consider walking one of the healthiest exercises you can do. It also gets me out in nature (which makes it a double de-stressor). Add listening to music on a walk...I have a stress releasing paradise! Plus, it helps me stay in shape, too – a while back, I was able to lose 103 pounds (over the course of a few years) from walking and watching what I ate.

Even if you exercise for just a few minutes. Make sure you stay active to get your blood pumping. Even light exercises, like Yoga which I will talk about in the next section, are very beneficial to your health, your stress levels, and your overall well-being.

Yoga

While it is physical in nature, Yoga is a spiritual practice that brings your mind and body together in harmony.

Yoga combines physical movement, breathing and meditation to benefit your overall health and well-being while helping you to release stress, too.

Yoga is another one of my favorite exercises because it helps me stretch, gain range of motion in my body, helps me focus on my breath and most importantly, helps me relax.

One of my favorite things about Yoga is there are different poses with varying types of difficulty. If you can't do one or a few poses, there is more than likely a pose or two that you can do. Plus, the more you do Yoga, the more poses you can work up to doing as your balance and flexibility will improve.

Progressive Muscle Relaxation

This is a technique that helps you lower stress and tension levels. It is a practice where you tense different muscle groups in your body and then relax them. Once your muscles are in a relaxed state, pay attention to what the muscle *feels* like when it is relaxed. This is to help you understand and recognize what it feels like for your muscles to be relaxed – opposed to being tense.

Here's how to do it:

1. Sit comfortably. It is best not to lie down because the purpose of this exercise is to help you notice what it feels like to relax while you are awake, and you don't want to fall asleep accidentally.

2. Take five, slow dep breaths.

3. Choose a muscle to tense, first – Magellan Healthcare recommends to "[s]tart with your facial muscles then move on to other muscle groups—neck, shoulders, arms,

chest, stomach, legs and feet—for full-body relaxation.".

4. After tensing the muscle for about five seconds, exhale, and release the tension in the muscle you chose.

5. Become aware of what it feels like to have the muscle be relaxed.

As you practice relaxing your muscles, over time, your goal is to recognize what it feels like for your muscles to be relaxed so you can learn to release the tension whenever you feel that your muscles are tensing up.

Cooking and Baking

When I was growing up, I was privileged to have a family that taught me how to cook. And cook well. Through my grandfather and father, not only did I learn *how* to cook, but also how to love and appreciate the art.

Over the years, as I grew to love cooking, I realized that not only do I love it, I love how it *relaxes* me when I cook. In fact, I try to cook dinner almost every day as part of my stress releasing routine. To me, cooking is like conducting a symphony of aromas and flavors and when you marry the ingredients together and add *love* to your food, you come out with a great meal that satisfies the mind, body and soul.

Yes, I said put love into your food because it is the most important ingredient! Remember, good food *always* needs love. You can actually taste it when someone just throws something together, tosses it on a plate and gives it to you. You can't taste the love in that.

While I know some people may think that cooking is a chore, for many, the process can be therapeutic. Cooking helps your mental state of being because it takes your mind off of the day and helps you concentrate on a task. It helps you physically because it keeps you active, grabbing ingredients, chopping, stirring, grabbing pots and pans out of the cupboards, etc. Plus, it helps you emotionally, because of the satisfaction you have that you made something, and it allows you to be as creative as you want.

If cooking isn't your thing, perhaps you like to bake, instead? Baking is another art – another form of creativity. Baking is practically the same thing as cooking in terms of the mental, emotional, and physical aspects of your well-being. However, it is an entirely different beast because measurements need to be exact. I'm not much of a baker, but I do bake from time to time and decorating cakes is one of my favorite baking activities.

Gardening

We have already talked about the benefits of being outdoors, but if you really want an activity that can give all the benefits of being outdoors, plus help you release stress in all dimensions of your well-being, gardening is a great activity.

Tending to plants can be very calming. Whether you are planting flowers in the spring, watering your garden, growing vegetables and feeling the accomplishment of growing your own food, and even pulling weeds to help your garden flourish, gardening can give you a multitude of benefits.

Gardening can be very grounding, calming, satisfying and can even be great exercise. If you've ever tended to your garden before, you know how gardening engages you physically and can be a great way to get your exercise in for the day.

CHAPTER SIX

Daily Rituals for A Balanced Life

"How do you prepare your mind and body for the task at hand? Establishing simple repeatable rituals can help." -Calm App Reflection

***

As you have read, stress can compromise our thoughts, feelings, and behaviors and when it becomes a chronic condition it can contribute to a variety of physical and mental health problems.

We know that nothing good comes from long-term stress. We also know taking care of ourselves is important. That means taking the time to unwind and relax is important for everyone to do every single day, too. However, most people do not make relaxing a priority.

How do you find time to manage it? Our to-do lists are never-ending. There's always going to be more to do than there is time in a day, and everything always takes 2x (more like 5x) longer than we think.

This is where setting up daily rituals to incorporate into your schedule - allowing you the time you need to relax - comes in.

According to Wellbeing People, "[n]ot only should we start our day feeling refreshed, but we should continue to refresh at various points throughout our day!". They say that even scheduling five minutes to unwind a few times throughout the day can be beneficial for you and help you de-stress and reenergize yourself.

If you start with taking short, five-minute breaks throughout your day to practice releasing stress, you are already making a positive impact on your health. In fact, I recommend creating a stress releasing routine, to help you create momentum with this positive change in your life.

Routine As Relaxation

As with any habit you want to form – in this case, creating a stress releasing habit – you need to create and adopt a routine. Multiple studies have shown that it takes 21 days to form a new habit.

As previously mentioned, starting with taking multiple five-minute breaks to release stress is a great start to incorporating relaxation in your daily life. If you want to try this method, try it out for 21 days and see how you feel.

A simple way to remind yourself to take your five-minute break is to set a couple of alarms on your phone throughout your day to remind you to de-stress for five minutes. Whether this is to sit with yourself for five minutes in a quiet location, to meditate for five minutes or sit down to breathe for five minutes, simply starting can make a huge difference to your health.

After practicing this for the recommended 21 days, it will start becoming a regular routine for you. Just remember that it can take *at least* 21 days to make this habitual for you. If it ends up taking 25 days, don't beat yourself up over it! Trust the process and continue to incorporate ways to release stress throughout your day.

If you want to start with something other than frequent five-minute breaks, go for it. This is about you and the best way for you to relax. If you like what you choose, make sure you try it out for 21 days to see if this can be a regular practice in your daily life.

Morning Routine

A Morning Routine is simply a ritual you can integrate into your schedule to start your day off on the right track. With a Morning Routine you can give yourself the opportunity connect with yourself, empower your day, and become unstoppable because you are starting your day out with minimal stress.

This is one of my favorite things to incorporate into my day. First, let me tell you, I am NOT a "morning person". I *need* my sleep! I'm sure some of you can relate. However, once I started to incorporate my Morning Routine into my day, I found that I felt *more* rested, felt like I had *more* time in my day, and I was able to *accomplish* more than I thought I could in one day.

Here is my sample Morning Routine:

4:30am-5:00am – Meditate for 20 minutes.
5:00am-6:00am – Exercise for 1 hour.
6:00am-7:00am – Read a book for 1 hour.
7:00am-8:00am – Shower, get ready for my day and eat breakfast.

I'm sure you noticed the start time and before you say anything, I repeat. I am NOT a morning person. I'm not here to convince you that waking up at 4:30am is something you should incorporate into your life, too. This is the time I chose to fit in a morning routine that I wanted into my life. This time fit in my life because I wanted to be able to meditate, exercise and read before I got ready for work.

The purpose of a Morning Routine is to choose activities you want to incorporate in your life to relax yourself before you start your day. To ease yourself into your day so you don't start the day with stress.

Think about it. Currently, you more than likely start your day with stress – waking up *late* to your alarm, getting ready as fast as you can, running out the door without eating breakfast and then dealing with morning traffic. Sounds pretty stressful!

Even if you woke up an hour to two hours earlier than your alarm, it's possible to ease yourself into your day and start off on the right foot. *Without* stress.

Tips For a Successful Morning Routine

- In the morning, we all have a habit of picking up our phones to check our emails, messages, Facebook, or anything else that compels you to check your phone in the morning. **STOP!** INSTEAD: look *outside* your window before you look at your device!

- Set an intention for your day by focusing on your vision for how you want the day to go. Then, think of one thing that will make you feel the most accomplished and free, and make a note to do that one thing.

- Drink water. Staying hydrated helps our bodies function better and properly, make sure you drink a few glasses of water, as our bodies are more dehydrated when we first wake up. Drinking water also helps reenergize you and improves your mental performance, to name a few more benefits.

- Move your body. Stretch, do some yoga, do your favorite exercise, whatever it is get your blood pumping.

- Meditate, or do a simple sitting exercise where you sit comfortably for 10 minutes and focus on your breath to clear your mind.

- Eat a healthy, balanced meal.

Of course, these are only tips about things that can help you set a positive tone for the day. You can choose to incorporate these things in your Morning Routine if you wish. Remember, your Morning Routine should comprise of anything that makes you feel relaxed enough to ease into your day.

Nighttime Routine

Same as a Morning Routine, a Nighttime Routine should be designed around releasing the stress that accumulated over the day. When you release stress from your day, you are more likely to sleep better throughout the night. A Nighttime Routine can be comprised of reading a book, meditating, deep breathing exercises, and/or taking a bath. Any of the techniques mentioned in this book are fair game.

For my own Nighttime Routine, I like to shake things up and work with different techniques, depending on the day I had. However, there is one thing that I incorporate into my ritual *every* night: I avoid blue light.

We are exposed to blue light on our phones, computers, tablets, TV's – basically anything with a screen – all day long. Not only do I do my best to protect my eyes from blue light throughout the day with blue light filters on my screens and by using blue light glasses, I stay away from blue light at least one hour before I go to bed. This is because blue light has been known to disrupt your sleep patterns as well as contribute to a list of health problems.

According to UCDavisHealth, "[e]xposure to blue light before bedtime also can disrupt sleep patterns as it affects when our bodies create melatonin. Interruption of the circadian system plays a role in the development of type 2 diabetes, cardiovascular disease, cancer, sleep disorders, and cognitive dysfunctions.".

Tips For a Successful Nighttime Routine

- Move your body. Stretch, do some light yoga, some stretching exercises or whatever light exercise that helps you feel calm and relaxed.

- Plan what you must do tomorrow and create a schedule for what you plan on accomplishing.

- Make any preparations you need for your Morning Routine - go over the Morning Routine you would like to incorporate or have already incorporated into your life.

- Practice gratitude. Smile and think of little signs, moments of joy and positive things that happened to you today, throughout the week and/or in your life so you can be more thankful, feel grateful and feel appreciation for these things. When you practice gratitude, it can help you recognize the good things in your life which can also help your mind and body.

As with your Morning Routine, these are suggestions as to what you can do before you go to bed. Remember, the point of a

Nighttime Routine is to relax yourself enough so you can ease yourself into a sound and pleasant sleep throughout the night.

Why Sleep is Important for Stress Relief

It is important to mention that sleep, in general, is important to your health. In terms of stress relief, sleep helps reduce cortisol and other stress hormone levels. Plus, when you are well rested, you are less likely to react strongly to negative situations that you may go through the next day.

This is why it is important to get the recommended amount of sleep per night. According to the Centers for Disease Control and Prevention, 13-18 year olds need 8-10 hours of sleep per night, adults 18-60 years old need 7 or more hours per night, adults 61+64 need 7-9 hours per night and adults 65 yeas and older need 7-8 hours per night.

When you get at least the recommended amount of sleep you need per night, you are more likely to feel refreshed, alert and ready for the day.

Chapter Seven

Integrating Calm Into Your Life

"The time to relax is when you don't have time for it." -Sydney J. Harris

***

Needless to say, nothing good comes from long-term stress! But, how do you find time to manage it? Our to-do lists are never-ending, there's always going to be more things to do than there is time in a day, and everything always takes 2x (more like 5x) longer than we think.

Sure, all of this is true, but if you put things in perspective and think of life as a journey, or a marathon, we can see that we simply cannot get everything done all at once or in the time "we need it to". Knowing that we can't finish everything that is thrown at us, we should be able to see that we should make time to work on things that are most important, like *taking care of ourselves*.

As you have read, staying stressed is what causes damage to our health. Chuck Pagano once said, "If you don't have your health, you don't have anything.". I'll let that sit with you as you think about the things you "need to do" today. Is taking care of yourself on that list? I'm guessing that if it isn't, you are thinking it should be.

Sure, our world is stressful. Of course we are going to get stressed from time to time. The important takeaway is that you need to find a way to integrate "calm" into your daily life in order to manage your stress levels. This is something, mandatory, that you must work on every day.

This means that managing the stressors in your life should be something that you work around and not work to incorporate. Integrating calm into your life means that you simply need to add it to the TOP of your to-do list and make sure that this is *the* most important task you need to accomplish every day.

Building a Personal Stress Management Plan

In order to integrate calm into your life, it's a good idea to build a Stress Management plan so that you will know how to react during stressful situations, or what you need to do once you start to feel stress.

First, when creating your Stress Management plan, identify what triggers your stress levels going up. Starting a stress journal to record what makes you stressed is a good idea to help you keep track of your stressors. If you notice you can't seem to shake the stress and it starts to linger, take note of it.

Something else to write down in your stress journal are the unhealthy ways you deal with stress. Some people stress-eat (like me - sometimes I "need" my "comfort food" and am always working on trying to avoid eating unhealthy foods when I'm stressed), some people drink too much, use drugs or smoke too much. Note the unhealthy ways you deal with stress in your stress journal so you can identify ways to cut these unhealthy habits out of your life.

Then, once you have assessed where your stress comes from and the unhealthy habits you may have adopted, brainstorm or try out some of the techniques mentioned in this book to see which technique(s) help you release stress from your body.

If you are not sure which ones to start with, choose your favorite technique and try it out. See how it works to release stress and calm you down. If you end up feeling more stressed, try another technique. The goal is to assess your own needs and preferences to find out the best solution for you.

Once you try out some stress releasing techniques, pay attention to which methods work best for you and take note of which ones work, and how. Pretty soon you will start seeing patterns of which techniques work best, and when. After a while you will be able to point out your "go-to" techniques and use these to create your Stress Management plan.

You are the only one who knows your body and knows your stress levels, too. Use the mindfulness techniques mentioned in this book to listen to your body and feel which techniques work best to release stress and make you feel better, overall.

Building a Sustainable Plan

Building a sustainable plan will give you the best chances of success to incorporate stress releasing techniques into your daily life that will become habits for you.

In order to build a sustainable plan, make sure you feel good about the techniques you are incorporating into your life. Also, just like exercising, make sure you *like* the techniques you incorporate into your life. If you don't feel good, the techniques make you more stressed instead of less, and/or don't like the techniques you are incorporating into your life, it will be harder to act on them every single day.

On that note, do what works for you. Don't do what a friend or family member does to help them release stress, chances are it won't work for you. If you want to try what they suggest, go ahead and try it. However, only incorporate it into your plan if it works to lower your stress levels.

Another way to make sure your plan is sustainable is to change things up every now and then. For example, say you chose to meditate every day for 21 days and it's starting to become a habit. Don't stop meditating and break the habit. Go with what's working for you (meditating) and shake things up by changing the *type* of meditation you choose to do every day. We talked about a few types of meditation such as a 20-minute inward meditation, Guided Imagery meditation and Palming meditation.

Tips for Consistency and Adaptability

Learning to take care of yourself and learning to listen to your body takes time. It is likely you won't get everything "right" how you need or expect it to be in one fell swoop. *This is ok.*

As long as you are trying and as long as you are taking small, productive steps towards making sure you release stress from your body, know you are doing just fine. If you find that something is not working, it is 100% ok to make adjustments to your plan. You are not stuck with the original plan you create. Again, work with what works for you. Don't become counterproductive by stressing yourself out trying to find out how to introduce calm into your life every day.

The most important thing to remember is if you don't feel the stress go away all at once, or if you are trying to make stress releasing a habit and miss a day out of the 21 days, or if you choose to use a technique that makes you even more stressed, don't beat yourself up about it. You are trying to make an overall, positive change for your body and for your life.

Trying to find out how to reduce stress and introduce calm into your life is more of a marathon - not a sprint. Small steps can lead to big changes and soon, you will find out what stress releasing technique(s) work best for you. All of this takes time, so give yourself some grace while working through the process.

Remember: it is the small little changes that make a big difference. Give yourself a break from stress because breaks now are better than breakdowns with your health later. You got this!

Conclusion

Mastering calm starts with the practice of being mindful about how we can manage our stress levels. As you have read, a small amount of stress is ok, but the goal is to not *stay* stressed as staying stressed is what causes damage to our bodies.

I hope my short pocket guide was enough to help motivate you towards making a positive change in your life that will be beneficial to your overall health and well-being.

If you found this book helpful, I'd be very appreciative if you would **leave a favorable review for this book on Amazon** so you can help others find this information to master calm in their lives, too.

Scan the above QR code to review.

References

5 ways being outdoors can make you healthier and happier | Sharp HealthCare. (2020, May 19). https://www.sharp.com/health-news/5-ways-being-outdoors-can-make-you-healthier-and-happier

A quote by Lao Tzu. (n.d.). https://www.goodreads.com/quotes/523350-if-you-are-depressed-you-are-living-in-the-past

Anthony, K. (2023, May 19). *Drinking water before bed.* Healthline. https://www.healthline.com/health/drinking-water-before-bed#negative-effects

Aromatherapy: Do essential oils really work? (2021, August 8). Johns Hopkins Medicine. https://www.hopkinsmedicine.org/health/wellness-and-prevention/aromatherapy-do-essential-oils-really-work#:~:text=Aromatherapy%20is%20the%20practice%20of,emotional%20center%20of%20the%20brain.

Bass, L. (2021, October 29). *Breathe It In: 11 Eucalyptus Oil Benefits.* Greatist.

https://greatist.com/health/eucalyptus-oil-benefits#:~:text=Some%20research%20shows%20that%20eucalyptus,were%20about%20to%20have%20surgery.

Benton, E. (2022, April 26). *The benefits of journaling for stress relief*. Psych Central. https://psychcentral.com/stress/how-to-begin-journaling-for-stress-relief#benefits-of-journaling

Burton, J., & Burton, J. (2023, August 16). *The Art of Stress Management: How to create less stress*. MQ Mental Health Research. https://www.mqmentalhealth.org/the-art-of-destressing-how-creativity-creates-less-stress/#:~:text=Focusing%20on%20the%20present%20moment,a%20hormone%20related%20to%20stress.

Calm, T. (2023, October 16). *Box breathing: how to do it and why it matters — Calm Blog*. Calm Blog. https://www.calm.com/blog/box-breathing#:~:text=Q%3A%20Why%20do%20Navy%20SEALs,and%20precise%20during%20critical%20operations.

Centerstone.org. (2023, May 9). *Good vs. Bad Stress | Processing & How to Cope with Stress*. Centerstone. https://centerstone.org/our-resources/health-wellness/good-vs-bad-stress/#:~:text=Examples%20of%20common%20positive%20stressors,perform%20well%20in%20the%20situation.

Clarabut, J. (2023, October 3). *Why relaxation is so important | Wellbeing People*. Wellbeing People. https://www.wellbeingpeople.com/2019/04/15/why-relaxation-i

s-so-important/#:~:text=When%20we%20relax%2C%20the%20fl
ow,blood%20pressure%20and%20relieves%20tension.

Coping with Stress. (n.d.).
https://www.cdc.gov/mentalhealth/cope-with-stress/index.html
#:~:text=Learning%20to%20cope%20with%20stress,energy%2C
%20desires%2C%20and%20interests.

Cosentino, B. W. (2021, April 20). *How Naps Can Keep You Happy and Healthy.* landmarkhealth.org. Retrieved November 11, 2023, from
https://www.landmarkhealth.org/resource/how-naps-can-keep-y
ou-happy-and-healthy/#:~:text=Naps%20increase%20energy%2
C%20improve%20reaction,and%20improve%20many%20cogniti
ve%20abilities.

Cultivating Health & UCDavisHealth. (2022, August 3). *How blue light affects your eyes, sleep, and health.* Cultivating Health. Retrieved November 14, 2023, from
https://health.ucdavis.edu/blog/cultivating-health/blue-light-eff
ects-on-your-eyes-sleep-and-health/2022/08#:~:text=How%20d
oes%20blue%20light%20affect,sleep%20disorders%2C%20and%2
0cognitive%20dysfunctions.

Definition of mindfulness. (2023). In *Merriam-Webster Dictionary.*
https://www.merriam-webster.com/dictionary/mindfulness

Exercise and stress: Get moving to manage stress. (2022, August 3). Mayo Clinic.
https://www.mayoclinic.org/healthy-lifestyle/stress-management

/in-depth/exercise-and-stress/art-20044469#:~:text=Examples%20include%20walking%2C%20stair%20climbing,a%20yoga%20video%20at%20home.

Fletcher, J. (2023, October 4). *How to use 4-7-8 breathing for anxiety.* https://www.medicalnewstoday.com/articles/324417#:~:text=The%204%2D7%2D8%20breathing,the%20practice%20of%20breath%20regulation.

Gray, A., & Gray, A. (2023, April 6). *How does music affect your mood and reduce stress.* PPL PRS. https://pplprs.co.uk/health-wellbeing/music-reduce-stress/#:~:text=All%20of%20this%20is%2C%20of,the%20mind%20and%20the%20body.

Harvard Health. (2020, July 6). *Understanding the stress response.* https://www.health.harvard.edu/staying-healthy/understanding-the-stress-response

How does sleep reduce stress? - Blog | Everlywell: Home Health Testing Made Easy. (n.d.). https://www.everlywell.com/blog/sleep-and-stress/how-does-sleep-reduce-stress/#:~:text=Better%20emotional%20regulation%20%E2%80%93%20When%20you,good%20night's%20sleep%20%5B11%5D.

How much sleep do I need? (2022, September 14). Centers for Disease Control and Prevention. https://www.cdc.gov/sleep/about_sleep/how_much_sleep.html

REFERENCES

How to do progressive muscle relaxation for anxiety. | Blog | Anxiety Canada. (2022, November 29). Anxiety Canada. https://www.anxietycanada.com/articles/how-to-do-progressive-muscle-relaxation/

Imagery. (2021, June 7). Johns Hopkins Medicine. https://www.hopkinsmedicine.org/health/wellness-and-preventi on/imagery#:~:text=Guided%20imagery.,beach%2C%20meadow %2C%20or%20forest.

King, B. (2020, January 20). *How Long Does It Take to Form A New Habit*. Psychology Today. Retrieved November 14, 2023, from https://www.psychologytoday.com/us/blog/taking-it-easy/2020 01/how-long-does-it-take-form-new-habit

Levo. (2023, September 22). *Stress Management: Incorporating mindfulness into your life*. Mile High Psychiatry. https://milehighpsychiatry.com/stress-management-incorporatin g-mindfulness-into-your-life/#:~:text=At%20its%20core%2C%2 0mindfulness%20is,greater%20sense%20of%20well%2Dbeing.

Mama, S. (2021, June 17). *How creativity can help you manage stress (and ways to get creative in your daily life)*. Source Mama. https://sourcemama.com.au/how-creativity-can-help-you-manag e-stress-and-ways-to-get-creative-in-your-daily-life/#:~:text=Bein g%20creative%20allows%20us%20to,feel%20in%20control%20an d%20calm.

Manage stress - MyHealthFinder | Health.gov. (2021, August 1). https://health.gov/myhealthfinder/health-conditions/heart-healt

h/manage-stress#:~:text=Overview,high%20blood%20pressure%2C%20and%20depression.

MEA | Search Result. (n.d.). Ministry of External Affairs, Government of India. https://www.mea.gov.in/search-result.htm?25096/Yoga:_su_origen,_historia_y_desarrollo#:~:text=Introduction%20%3AYoga%20is%20essentially%20a,'%20or%20'to%20unite'.

Mindfulness exercises. (2022, October 11). Mayo Clinic. https://www.mayoclinic.org/healthy-lifestyle/consumer-health/in-depth/mindfulness-exercises/art-20046356

Mindfulness meditation: A research-proven way to reduce stress. (2019, October 30). *https://www.apa.org*. https://www.apa.org/topics/mindfulness/meditation#:~:text=Researchers%20believe%20the%20benefits%20of,downstream%20effects%20throughout%20the%20body.

Nunez, K. (2023, June 12). Should you be drinking water first thing in the morning? Here are 6 healthy perks, according to MDs. *Real Simple*. https://www.realsimple.com/health/preventative-health/benefits-of-drinking-water-in-morning#:~:text=%22Drinking%20water%20when%20you%20wake,the%20night%20before%2C%20he%20adds.

Practicing gratitude. (2022, July 25). NIH News in Health. https://newsinhealth.nih.gov/2019/03/practicing-gratitude#:~:text=When%20you%20make%20gratitude%20a,positive%20emotion%20that%20you%20experience.

REFERENCES

Professional, C. C. M. (n.d.). *Stress*. Cleveland Clinic. https://my.clevelandclinic.org/health/articles/11874-stress

Relaxation techniques for health. (n.d.). NCCIH. https://www.nccih.nih.gov/health/relaxation-techniques-what-you-need-to-know#:~:text=Relaxation%20techniques%20are%20practices%20to,opposite%20of%20the%20stress%20response.

Releasing Stress through the power of Music | Counseling Services. (n.d.). University of Nevada, Reno. https://www.unr.edu/counseling/virtual-relaxation-room/releasing-stress-through-the-power-of-music

Robinson, L. (2023a, February 28). *Laughter is the Best Medicine*. HelpGuide.org. https://www.helpguide.org/articles/mental-health/laughter-is-the-best-medicine.htm#:~:text=A%20good%2C%20hearty%20laugh%20relieves,improving%20your%20resistance%20to%20disease.

Robinson, L. (2023b, October 11). *Stress Management: How to reduce and Relieve stress*. HelpGuide.org. https://www.helpguide.org/articles/stress/stress-management.htm

Scott, E., PhD. (2023, October 22). *How to power nap for your mental health*. Verywell Mind. https://www.verywellmind.com/power-napping-health-benefits-and-tips-stress-3144702

Shannon. (2022, July 20). *How self-awareness reduces stress*. Brightside.

https://www.brightside.com/blog/how-self-awareness-reduces-stress/#:~:text=By%20being%20self%2Daware%2C%20you,to%20resolve%20or%20manage%20it.

Smith, M., MA. (2023, November 14). *Guided imagery meditation*. HelpGuide.org. https://www.helpguide.org/meditations/guided-imagery-meditation.htm#:~:text=Guided%20imagery%20is%20a%20relaxation,peaceful%20scene%20in%20your%20mind.

Stress symptoms: Effects on your body and behavior. (2023, August 10). Mayo Clinic. https://www.mayoclinic.org/healthy-lifestyle/stress-management/in-depth/stress-symptoms/art-20050987#:~:text=Common%20effects%20of%20stress&text=Stress%20that's%20not%20dealt%20with,%2C%20stroke%2C%20obesity%20and%20diabetes.

Summer, J., & Summer, J. (2023, November 2). *Napping: benefits and tips*. Sleep Foundation. https://www.sleepfoundation.org/sleep-hygiene/napping#:~:text=In%20general%2C%20the%20best%20nap,grogginess%20and%20actually%20worsen%20sleepiness.

The healing power of nature – hidden river healing. (n.d.). https://hiddenriverhealing.com/the-healing-power-of-nature/#:~:text=It%20comforts%20us%20and%20calms,Quite%20simply%2C%20nature%20is%20restorative.

The Importance of Relaxing. (2016). *Momentum Finding Time to Unwind*. Retrieved November 11, 2023, from https://beingwell.yale.edu/sites/default/files/files/2016%20July%20Momentum%20Yale.pdf

The Power of Rituals: How to Build Meaningful Habits | By Gustavo Razzetti. (n.d.). https://www.fearlessculture.design/blog-posts/the-power-of-rituals-how-to-build-meaningful-habits#:~:text=%E2%80%9CWe%20see%20in%20every%20culture,reduce%20anxiety%20and%20increase%20confidence.

Tuckett, S. (2022, December 19). *The impact of music on the nervous system and mental health.* sarahtuckett.com.au. https://sarahtuckett.com.au/the-impact-of-music-on-the-nervous-system/

WebMD Editorial Contributors. (2021, April 9). *What is box breathing?* WebMD. https://www.webmd.com/balance/what-is-box-breathing

Weingus, L. (2023, January 12). *30 journaling prompts for stress relief.* Silk + Sonder. https://www.silkandsonder.com/blogs/news/journal-prompts-for-stress-relief

Printed in Great Britain
by Amazon